thirds

For Jane —

With love and
best wishes —

Bill, Charlene & Hattie

7-4-92

thirds

Charles Rossiter
William Schmidtkunz
Jeffrey Winke

Distant Thunder Press
Madison, Wisconsin

Copyright (c) 1985 by Distant Thunder Press

Some of these poems have previously appeared in *Bonsai, Bugle American, Cicada, Dragonfly, Frogpond, HIGH/COO, Modern Haiku, Third Coast Archives, Third Coast Haiku Anthology* and *Wind Chimes*.

Also: *Dreams of Meaning*, C. Rossiter, Milwaukee: House of Words, 1978.

Mountain Talk, Jusan Atnarko (William Schmidtkunz), Milwaukee: Distant Thunder Press, 1979.

Just Enough, Jeffrey Winke, Milwaukee: House of Words, 1977.

Library of Congress Number: 85-70935
ISBN: 0-9614525-0-1

DISTANT THUNDER PRESS
1007 Sunnyvale Lane, Suite E
Madison, Wisconsin 53713

Preface

"A haiku is the expression of a temporary enlightenment, in which we see into the life of things."
—R. H. Blyth

<u>Thirds</u> is a testament to friendship. Spread out over the United States, the three of us have remained friends over the years through hundreds of letters, a few visits, a number of telephone calls and many, many haiku. Whether written on the back of dime store postcards, scribbled on a page torn from the notebook, jotted down on diner napkins or neatly typed on a page, we have found the power of haiku has enabled us to share feelings, experiences and events with economy of words.

For those who are not familiar with haiku, a haiku is generally considered to be a "breath length" poem. It is based on the idea that the pure emotional impact of an experience lasts for only a moment. To enjoy haiku, it is best to approach them in a contemplative mood, since haiku invite readers to "complete" them by relating the feeling expressed to their own experiences. In a way, reading haiku is as much an art as writing them.

The three of us hope that <u>Thirds</u> will prove to be stimulating reading for both the novice and expert haiku reader.

CR
WS
JW

Charles Rossiter is an independent scholar and freelance writer living in Washington, D.C. He also teaches courses on the Beat poets, creativity and interpersonal communication.

William Schmidtkunz spends his summers farming in Sutton, Alaska and his winters as part of an oil exploration team on Alaska's north slope.

Jeffrey Winke is a business writer and manager of Corporate Communications for a Madison, Wisconsin mortgage insurance company. He is also the associate editor of the magazine Modern Haiku.

Charles Rossiter

*silent moon-filled night,
a thousand sand grains move
to make this footprint*

*three empty boxcars
stand in an open field;
SOO LINE   SOO LINE   SOO LINE*

*ribbon of mist,
winds among the warehouses;
the frozen river*

eleven p.m.,
    twenty-five below zero,
        walking with Joe

*as she walks away
thighs almost touching
the setting sun*

*blue silo
with peeling white letters:
"drink milk for health"*

*empty field—
four black horses
in drizzling rain*

*lone jogger,
another lone jogger,
two more up there*

april mistymorn . . .
fishwishers alluring, plunk
plunk   plunk
                plunk

*silver gills working
the rainbow tosses and flips—
on black asphalt*

*quiet evening
her shadow bends
across the bed*

*city night—
stroking the fur
of a stray cat*

*reading Basho,
the mournful strains
of Coltrane's horn*

sunday morning . . .
    one brown shoe
        beside the curb

*sudden thunder
the crying child
becomes still*

morning . . .
    a little brandy
        still in the snifter

dim gallery—
   a dead face
      smiles from the wall

*black monument—
a pale pair of hands
points to a name*

plucked so gently
*   yet three petals fall—*
autumn rose

Nan's back yard:
my old high chair
rusting away

William Schmidtkunz

the small scar
on her cheek
a dimple when she smiles

*home from the hike
poking stove ashes
for the baked potatoes*

*hoeing weeds
my garden shoes
ready for the compost*

*monarchs
or autumn leaves—
who can tell this windy day?*

*spider's egg sac
in the claw
my dead grandfather's hammer*

*turning the garden
and a piece of sky!
the broken mirror*

*perched
on a juniper limb
black crow and crescent moon*

*twilight...
the steady rain
on the barking dog*

snow dune
a frozen windfist
punches blue sky

*incinerator man
the old janitor's face
ablaze by the open door*

*warming hands
on exhaust pipes
the burning gloves*

*a plate of cut apples
turning brown in the sunny window,
and the old woman*

an armadillo?
but we're not in Mexico!
the old recap on the road

last sun of the day
my long bent shadow
across the half spaded garden

*opening
the empty root cellar—
smelling last year's potatoes*

*and the ship pulls up
the rusty anchor, and the anchor
a rusty moon*

*winter, yet still clinging
the setting sun — the ripest apple
in the orchard*

old growth cottonwood
now a yellow sawdust trail
into the woodshed

*another deep snow
only a smoking prayer stick
holds up my hut*

*journey's beginning
will the snow never melt
from my path?*

Jeffrey Winke

*into the moon
circles in circle
the stone sinking . . .*

darkness.
a mountain appears　　　*disappears*
quick as the lightning

*cold spring wind
her blouse cuts
a soft shape*

farmers market:
   the way the sun
      reddens the rhubarb

         new corn shoots
         those under the tree's reach
         a paler green

casting shadows
where the sun cannot light
row of pine

*alone . . .
on the red horizon
one red barn*

*winter
one leaf clings—
the cocoon*

*face full of snow
. . . and still grinning
terra cotta gargoyle*

white noise
in the white computer room
a vase of red roses

whisper of a breeze:
her sentiment expressed
with a touch

*in the crowded bar—
somewhere—
my blind friend*

another whiskey
even the trophy trout
swims

*a cloud shifts
my shadow is cast
in the canyon*

        *layers of clouds
        the sun sets . . . then appears
        above the horizon*

drizzling . . .
black gents on the porch
two with sunglasses

*song birds
at train yard's edge,
two cars coupling*

warm bath . . .
the sound of the overflow
her pregnant belly still dry

*in cold shadows
behind the station
leaves circling*

```
                              o
                              n
                              e

                              s
                              m
                    s         o
                    t         k
          s         a         i
          m         c         n
 f        o         k         g
 o        k         s
 u        e
 r
```

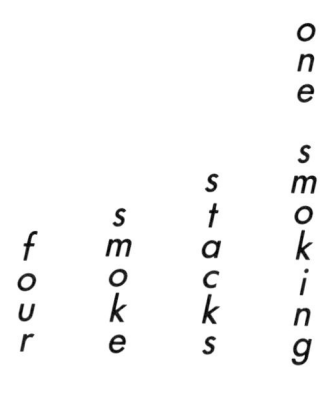